CEPHALOPRESS

www.cephalopress.com

i

Published in the UK by Cephalopress Ltd 2019

www.cephalopress.com
info@cephalopress.com

Copyright © Elisabeth Horan

Spanish edited by John Homan and Jorge Montero Calderón

Cover Design by Daniel Lambert

Book design by Cephalopress Ltd

ii

SELF-PORTRAIT

BY ELISABETH HORAN

CONTENTS

For Frida

I paint self-portraits because I am so often alone, because I am the person I know best.

- Frida Kahlo

Dear Reader,

I am very honored for you to be holding this book in your hands. Thank you.

To give you an insight into this work, Frida Kahlo has long been a heroine and inspiration to me, both as an artist and a woman. I have studied her throughout my life and academic career and always wanted to write poems about her in some fashion.

Frida kept making her art, right up till the end, even from her bed, when she was in too much pain to rise. With her speaking to me, I created these poems during a long and tumultuous recovery in a bed of my own. So you will see the threads I tried to weave into the manuscript: the accident, her deep love and loyalty to Diego Rivera, the tumultuous ups and downs of their marriage, her own reckonings with her sexuality and place in society as a woman, an artist and a Mexican, and the deep physical and psychological scars from the tragedy which she carried with her the rest of her life. I tried very hard to honor her memory and legacy respectfully, but to also dig into the core of her heart and psyche, with the gifts of her portraits as clues to what her experience was really like.

I am not a Latina woman, and do not endeavor to know the Mexican experience as my own, but I have lived and studied and worked in Mexico and at various points in my life have considered it my home. I do realize the sensitivity of that side of this work.

I think this is a time in our world where women and humans everywhere could use a collection of a woman who defied such odds to survive and still created such masterpieces.

Kahlo brings me into her folds, into the womb of sisterhood, into the rich earth of mother nature and into the circle of pain and survival which we, as women, find in each other.

I truly hope you enjoy the poems.

Elisabeth

CRASH SONNET
1925

The trolley or the bus; Zona Rosa
O Colegio, Alejandro y yo; his hand   *Alejandro and me*
On my knee - my eyes on his lips;
My hand on his cheek - my future in
His kiss - choqué choqué - ya no nos   *crash, crash - now we don't*
Besamos, instead feel this bone   *kiss,*
Poking out, feel this lesion or blood
Flowing out of my back or my
Abdomen; imagine me like I was
Before, Alejandro, when I was whole,
And you kissed me on the bus or trolley;
Your hand on my knee or shoulder;
My future as your wife, erased in a second -
Choqué, choqué - ya me mató.   *crash, crash - now I am dead.*

3

COYOACÁN
1925

No one knows the breaking
As I know the breaking of glass
It is the shards which get at you, you
Know, not so much the steel rods
Or the splintered wood; those do
Horrible things to human tissue

But the shards, the shards, have a
Way they get into the insides into
Veins in capillaries under toenails
The mucous membranes, the eyelids
Might be the worst thing they do

The nurses come and I tell them.
I say: *ayúdame, no puedo ver*   *help me, I can't see*
Ni la luz de la ciudad   *the lights of the city*
Ni la de la vida   *nor those of the living*

They say: *no hay nada más allá, adentro*

            there is nothing left in there

Frida; there is no more glass in your
Eye; there is nothing, nothing in there
Querida   *my dear*

Life begins tomorrow,
People like to say, because
They will have children - and they

Are not yet deceased - they have
No shards of glass in their eyes, nor
The steel metal rod implanted like a
Crude IUD in my uterus.

Tu Botticelli
1926

For Alejandro

Soy tu Botticelli   *I am your Botticelli*
perpetrator de pérdidas   *perpetrator of loss*
aunque ya no eres mío   *even though you are no longer mine to lose*

Europe and its mothers
tend to be bitches; scold
and take their babies away

To high art places:
duomos, cathedrals -
curators of good types of women.

I am the cala; the German witch -
all Mexican: little dove; little monkey;

La mezcla Tehuana   *the native mix of Tehuana*
not so refined some say;

Who says -
Quien dice -   *who says -*
Qué dice la selva?   *and what says the jungle?*

The lust within me works much better
no como mis piernas rotas;   *not like my broken legs;*
Las que corrían;   *which used to run to you;*

The ones killing you with desire,
wrapped around your body,

My meat would arrive - along with your hunger
mi carne llegará - con tu hambre

Quiero asfixiarte con amor.   *I want to smother you with my love.*

Fey
1929

I love the way
He looked at me

Mirándome	*gazing at me*
Como si fuera	*as if I was*

Chocolate o un dulce	*chocolate or a candy*
Beautiful young woman	

Of 23
Staring over a balcony

At her mentor to be
As he imagined the woman's nipple in his

Mouth
I pretended, instead, that he was painting me

She was older
As one day I would be

I never knew that I would change - so
Drastically

From a small young flower
To a scarred and half-broken tree

God, if you knew -
what was to become of me -

Would you have turned the bus?
Stopped the wheels of the trolley?

Not sent me out that day
A reunirme con Alejandro   *to meet up with my boyfriend*

Para comer   *to eat*
Y disfrutar   *and enjoy*

Con mi novio   *with my love*
En la Ciudad   *in the city*

El arte, la música, la gente   *the art, the music, the people*
Todo brillando a nuestro alrededor   *everything around us shining*

Viviendo   *living*
Y yo   *and me*

On my way to hell
Al diablo -   *to the devil -*

On my way to hurt
La pérdida   *the loss*

On my way to destroy
La fe   *the faith*

Que me había tenido -   *which I had had -*
Encima de eso   *and on top of that*

On my way to marrying you -

Pinche loco   *fucking crazy*
Amor de mi vida.   *love of my life.*

Diego Rivera:
Mi otro accidente.   *my other accident.*

MOLE POBLANO
1929

Chocolate y chile
My breasts and my ass

Sensual spice
Cheating comes the day's grace

Poor babies
Like nopales

Chopped drunken
From the womb

De Puebla-
No walking comes

From the Revolución
Only running

And for success, las señoras
De Diego - deberían   *Diego's women ought to*

Reunirse como amigas, porque   *unite themselves as friends,*
Qué más qué hacer?   *for what else is there to do?*

Que prepararle   *than to make him*
Muy buenas tortillas.   *delicious tortillas.*

Empty Banner
1930

Anarchy is just fine -
take a lap around the pool
taste the other types of water

Travel communists
need linguists

Need your short bob -
like my cupid doll -

Canary on a balcony.
Marx knows, I know

The way a woman's tongue can do
things golden dust cannot

Skeleton tape - beware -
come visit me not in San Francisco -
no te permito seguirme ahí   *I do not allow you to pursue me there*

There - I long to hiss along her back
be a bone in her vagina

You know her
you know about syringes

Body cast imprints
catheters; orgasms

La Serpiente Verde -   *the green serpent -*

Within this skin
little blue bird

Sparkled as sky
flies home to D.F.

Without having said
goodbye.

How I Like to Imagine Diego
1931

There is nothing I can't touch.
Your torso de Apollo

Black walls of lace surround me
no hay nada que no toco   *there is nothing I won't touch*

Después de saberte mío   *after knowing of you as mine*
el viejo está cansado   *so tired is the old man*

Veiled and burning
my virgin eyes

No hay nada más que hacer   *here is nothing left for my body to do*
que postrarme a tus pies   *than lay prone at your feet*

A sin for you to touch my legs, yet
treason to pull away

Plunge the hand in merciless
close the creaking puerta del amor   *door of love*

Serrate me windworn
back and forth

Deeply, mi rostro herido   *wounded is my face*
la piel cortada, abierta   *with skin, cut and open*

17

Desnuda por sus palabras   *stripped naked by your words*
I bleed, I fall, me estás matando   *you are killing me*

I'm just a thing for touching
my death muy, muy pequeña   *my very little, little death*

No me queda más que hacer   *there is nothing left for me to do*
ya que soy tu flor pequeña   *I am your little flower*

Me matas para amarme   *you kill me for to love me*
I touch your insides, every word

My eyes veiled, on fire, ten
little toes plied & curled.

PROYECTO PARA REPARARME EN TRES ETAPAS, VOL. 1
1931

Uno.

S spine
Not x spine
Chucked
Not good sleeping
Or babies spine
Chunks
Of it in the road
Not ideal
Street cars... Trollies
Whatever the term

Frida, artist, poet, man, woman
Whatever the term

Prodigee (prodigy or protégée?)
Mentor
Terms. Terms.

Debatable who's who
Debatable which disk
Fucked worse
Which mentee
Broken worse
When metal meets

Columns

De hueso o de piel	*of bone or of skin*
Look lo que se perdió	*look at what is lost*
Son partes humanas	*it's pieces of a human*
No de naciones industrializadas	*not of industrialized nations*
O. La pérdida.	*o. the loss.*

Dos.

So, that done -
Discussed.
I had a finger - a
Special one.
It runs along
Broke tracks
It glues and
Binds shatter
Chips and
Crunched
Bones back
As sinew might
Lap itself as a
Kitten might
Run herself
Along your leg
Or crutch
I slide a tongue
Or finger along the
Zag, and it
Doesn't change

Broken tracks,
But it does
Numb -
And make me forget -
And oh. How
This lithe bone
Of love
Is itching
To distract.

Tres.

Mentor
Make a mural then
Mentor
Make the black fishes swim
Mentee traces a new spine
A new canvas back

All you need are the colors
Of my blood
The smell of
My flowers
And the ocean
Of woman

Pain.
So circumstantial.

As the body is

Tethered to the
Choices it makes -

Not all orgasms
Need be rational,
Nor physical.

Proyecto Para Repararme en Tres Etapas, Vol. 2
1931

I

I dream about the time
You might have painted
My nipple, and my spine
Aligns - that I might sit
Straight or recline, arching
Perfectly at the waist - as
I saw done by the others.

II

It was all about the angle;
Your view.

III

And I am not,
Nor will I ever be -
Disabled for you.

No Puedo Parar (I Can't Stop)
1932

What they told me to do
was to make a hole
and then I would reach in
and pull out
a bouncing baby boy,

El mío   *mine*

but if I pulled too hard, he,
(The Red Snake),
would also come out and
eat the baby,

El mío   *mine*

so when I went in to tug
I was very hesitant, and
I claim that it's their fault
you see,

El suyo   *theirs*

if they had told me
to just go for it -
to just fucking yank that
son of a bitch
by his foot or ass or head

or whatever

Es mío   *mine*

I could have grabbed
onto him as a handle
and then this would not be this...

you see - instead this would be
a nightmare

Es suyo   *theirs*

in which God punishes me,
and I instead would be nursing
a bouncing baby boy

Era mío   *was mine*

and I would not be bled dry with

                        a gaping hole

and the staples
and the lake of crimson
on which I slide along
always feet first -

Era mío   *was mine*

legs spread, ovaries trailing,
useless - like jellyfish,
toward the vast and merciless
women's ocean -
full of dead fish.

Cuando Pierdo (When I Lose) 1932

Balloons of blood they are supposed to be
Pinche anvil / Chingada mujer   *fucking anvil / fucked woman*

Blood balloons carry your life inside me
La flor fea / El hijo mío   *the ugly flower / the son of mine*

I do not work
I do not produce living things

Things like high art can be a human fetus
Out of the womb

See how long he can writhe
Under a doctor's thumb

So vain, and so dumb;
The doctors with their glib tongues…

Do they think I do not hear their whispers!?
Oh, so sad, la Señora de Rivera

(what a situation)

Lucky artist, lucky wife, lucky half-monkey
What an abomination-woman.
There are ghouls in the tubes

They make worse the son;
They hold him under a
Pillow till the heartbeat gone,

(then eject him)

As if a raisin, a hideous grape - the tannins
Not within him, but running torrential down

My legs - would you wish this upon
Anyone - even someone who comes,

Cómo lo habría hecho yo?   *like I have done?*
Eyaculando   *ejaculating*
Putrid paint upon her deformed tree - splashing

Ochers and greens as if she were free
From the masses - free from God.

Pero, ella no está libre -   *but, she is not free -*
Confía en mi.   *trust in me.*

She creates dead things - hair
From dead horses -

And shrunken heads,
And shrunken heads -

From deep within the festering pools
Of her womb like a slurry.

Look at this Face Coming Out of my Vagina
1930

This is my face - look at it.

Can you see me?
It's not very pretty.

Conoces a esta mujer?   *do you know this woman?*
The woman here?

Her face upon the wall,
In this room;

She is in this blue room
And upon its floor.

Do you see how there is a floor?
Beneath the bed:

The brown bed with
His two stupid brown feet?

And she is not me.

She is not in labor.
She is not losing a son,
Or a beautiful daughter

Lo sabias?   *did you guess - this?*

I am death's eyes
Coming out as a hideous smile

From between those legs,
Those horse thighs

Su cabeza fea -   *her ugly head -*
Y una vulva del diablo   *her evil vulva*

She calls you out as voyeur;
Ser impío; un hereje -   *blasphemous; heretic -*

This should prompt the end of the world:
When we are killing what we recognize:

A vagina forced to expel:

That which it cannot protect.
That which it cannot heal.

EN EL HOSPITAL, VOL 1
1932

All the things come back to me
Even as they float away in a red tide
Of blood
It isn't menstrual
This death slide
Not at all -
The tears I cry - are menstrual
This is more like
The unnatural
Tears of my insides
The smile of a nurse
Her hand on my shoulder
Cryptic shape of a pelvis
Almost like a jail
In a way really looks like
A man's shoulders
Slow death trail
Slime of a selfish snail
Trailing away
With its house
And perhaps my baby -
Inside
Calcified -
My pubic hair
Is so ashamed to
Be in this painting
I don't listen

My face turns to you
I can't remember why
Maybe it was in prayer
Or maybe that's just
What it has become so very
Used to doing.

MATERNITY COFFIN
1932

It's the cries of dead babies at night.
Provoking mews; shrieks, gurgles,
hiccupping

As if I'd fed them
too much / or not enough milk.

So inane when
I've fed them blood and dirt and air -

Nadie llorando en mi pecho   *none of them crying at my breast*
ni sus lágrimas entrando   *nor their tears running*
en mi espacio -   *down my chest -*

Blood and syringes -
empty / full

This juxtaposition of
a life saved / a life ruined.

Soy media - mujer   *I am half of a woman*
llena / vacía   *full / empty*

Orgullosa, no con un hijo deforme   *proud, but not of the deformity*
en el útero - eso es -   *within me - this is -*

God's plan / What plan
allows for

This Eden / this Eve
to have her legs cut off?

El dolor es útil para saber mi destino -
the pain so useful; I understand my destiny -

See her scoot around the floor
on hips / on hands
as crutches.

Patética.   *pathetic.*

Cut her off half way down
above the legs / below the waist

Y ellos discuten que soy   *today they discuss me*
una ruina / una mujer ansiosa   *the ruin I am / the anxious woman*

Media fantasma - sin escoger   *half ghost - no choice*
quién me prefería diría "Pobre Frida…"

they love to utter "poor Frida…"

A woman's shape is
but the sum of her parts.

So mine gestates
a hacked triangle / backbone at an angle

36

In which
no ova finds solace.

Corro a un lugar   *I escape to a place*
donde esconden / donde entierran

                              where they hide / where they bury

Los cuerpos como   *bodies like*
el mío / y el de mi hijo   *mine / and like that of my son*

Do you know about this…?
This graveyard?

This ghost woman / maternity coffin?

I HATE THE WAY I LOOK
1933

When I roll the eyes inside my head
I see things I'm glad
you are not forced to - well,

this is mild compared
to the real inside of me -
that which I see.

Monster.

Failure.

Incompetent mother.

Not even a mother / a deformed monster.

Eater of hearts.

Defecator of hearts.

Proud Mexican.

Ashamed Mexican.

Comunista.

Animal.

Broken woman alone in bed.

Butterfly.

Green eyed viper watching over.

Sister of love.

Sister of hate.

Hater of men.

Lover of women.

Sexual.

Deformed animal.

Animal protector.

Soft bosom for resting small animals.

Temptress.

Hideous.

Ceniza del Volcán.   *ash from Popocatepetl.*

Fénix de Coyoacán.   *phoenix of Coyoacán.*

Heart in hands.

Heart detached from chest.

No longer pulsing

Bloody in.

Bloody out

So tired

Yet never resting.

SMALL THINGS
1935

You can see that my breasts are available to the casual onlooker even if the man who killed me doesn't want others to see, they are remaining available - this is something society does - men do - to women; they make me available, accessible, without us even knowing, we are on view to many people - they do - some do - they sometimes hide the pubic area - but only partly, maybe you can still see it and it remains erotic to many.

Despite being dead, and I am really, really dead; on the news they said it was just "little nips" which he gave me, sounded like some kind of after dinner drink, but no, it was of el cuchillo I'm sure a sharp one at that, hunting or restaurant grade - and look how they let him stay in the room with me after. That's my murderer. Not that he is any danger to me now, but it seems they could ask him to leave and quickly throw a white sheet over.

Este cuerpo - this body is no good for anything - who would even want it - it won't work again. It would be hurtful for many children. Too many punctures, too much blood loss for sure. What a mess for someone to clean up, even the edges tainted by the snake - I see. You are not happy with this. This description. I am just relaying to you what I saw them report on TV.

La Leche
1937

Mothers sometimes make no milk
Sometimes not enough, or tainted
With alcohol, spousal abuse - and the like

I never had enough,
It seems, of children;
You can borrow a uterus,
But it's pricey and it's personal

A breast is a breast is a breast;
Is a way to keep babies alive -
You can give them cow's milk and sugar,
Or a slurry of oats or maize

It's the lactic acid they prefer.
It's the woman with a healthy
Reproductive system I would
Prefer to be. Why do I need a

Foot if I cannot pull a cart like an ox -
Why would I need my heart -
If it is to be chopped up
Between two people and drained.

Cold and blue in the lonely blue house.
Her breast was brown, the nipple
Purple; the milk warm and perfect;

The dribble... inevitable.

Ya no era de bebé   *and I was no longer a baby*
Ni era yo de niña   *and I was no longer a girl*

But always drinking more milk,
Unable to produce my own

Nor mutate into a mother,
Nor wear any sort of prideful
Smile - ever.

HOLE IN CHEST WITH ARROW
1937

Life is something I had with you
It doesn't matter which ulcer

        you choose

Her or me
Me or her
Love or agony
My body becomes
A trash yard

Pero mírala -   *yet look at her -*

Floreciendo como una mujer   *blossoming like a woman*
Más hermosa - más útil - para ti   *more lovely - more useful - for you*

She is so fragrant and youthful
I'm a gaping wound -

I bring three
Arms for three persons -

Pero mírala -   *yet look at her -*

A la Christina - piernas abiertas   *at this Christina - her open legs*
Walk toward you;

Her open mouth,
Opens ever wider;

Gaping over your face
She positions herself - arriba   *above*

Injects some venom
Into you - your cuerpo   *body*

Don't try to touch me like you used to do -
Rather touch me as if

I was more like her
Walking toward you
Legs spread open

Y mírala ahora   *and look at her now*

Skirt up over her head

Thin and loose, it undulates
In your face
As you begin to rub her -

Y mira como ella no esta   *and look how she is not*

Shot open
Like this V -
This arrow barb; mirame -   *look at me -*
I cannot pull it out of me -

My infection

Sinks deep, ever deeper
Into my deer meat.
The flies, the maggots -
I multiply till no flesh is left

For a school girl's branding;
Childish loss of virginity;

She is at once full of blood
She is at once exsanguinated

Her heart not the
Only thing on the ground

Once implantation fails -
Once the zygote
Is amputated.

Pero, mírala - mi hermana -	*yet look at her - my sister -*
Ya viene la virgen	*here comes the virgin*
Está abierta -	*her arms open*
Bailando, bailando - a ti	*dancing, dancing toward you*
Y mírame - tu viuda -	*and look at me - your widow -*
Piernas cerradas	*my legs closed*
Retirando, retirando - de ti	*retreating, retreating - away from you*

Aver, como te quedas tu -   *and now, look at you -*

Las manos decididas;   *expectant hands;*
Y tu cara que sonría -   *your smiling face -*

Contento. Abierto,   *content. open,*
Entre las dos hermanas.   *between two sisters.*

GRINGO DOLL
1937

There is a method.
I stare at your lens.
Oye Gringo: soy algo   *listen gringo: I am something*

Que debes ver, cómo tatuaje;   *you should see, like a tattoo;*
Diferente de cuantos   *so different than what you are*
Conozcas, que fascinante   *used to, so fascinating*

You're entranced by me
As if I were a monkey.
Or a woman naked, maybe
Displayed

Or a native Tehuana erotic
In some way - exotic
For you to gaze upon

No. I don't let you.
I don't shave my eyebrow; I let it
Bond with the other

Diego:
Mira amor, como me miran   *look honey, look how they view me*
Como si fuera exotic; erotic   *as if I was exotic; erotic*

Let them see you, Frida. Por Favor.
Please behave, Amor. Just be you.

49

Be beautiful. Let them adore you.
Be beautiful. Put the flowers in your
Hair. Weave. Weave. Sit there and stare.

Beautiful erotic; exotic
Tehuana... Pórtate bien.   *Tehuana... behave yourself.*
Look. And stare. Turn your

Face back
To the lens -
Así es. Házlo.   *this is how things are. just do it.*

Ah... mi vida.   *oh... my love.*
Manos. Mis manos,   *hands. my hands,*
Viviendo sobre tu cara   *living upon your visage*

There is a method.
I stare at your lens.
I sit in a chair
With my doll

The doll, white - as the gringo snow
Myself, and its facial hair
Inching toward its partner -
Two aching vines in the jungle.

I glare at your camera.
My hands in my lap.
Watching you covet
Esa mujer mezclada.   *this mixed woman.*

Y su tatuaje bien grabado.   *and her very deep tattoo.*

MI PROPIO ESPOSO (MY OWN SPOUSE)
1937

Por Fulang Chang   *For her monkey, Fulang Chang*

Dios me Dió   *God has gifted me*
El corazón roto   *a broken heart*

Drips a scarlet paint
Upon a beautiful canvas

See it curl into shapes - like
Beautiful hips and asses -

Dios me Dió   *God has given me*
Mis ganas de pintar   *my urge to make art*

I splay paint vermillion
Over your closed casket -

Igual que lo hacen los gusanos   *just like the worms go*
Through the valves
Through the guts, your heart

Dios no esta mirando   *God is not watching*
Lo que estoy haciendo   *what I am up to*

How I do this by myself
Para recrearme a mi misma   *to recreate myself*

Into a woman, into a monkey;
One who will love me, late at night -

As my own fucking husband -
De nuevo.   *who is always brand new.*

SE MARCHITÓ
1938

Para mis heroínas, Frida y Selena

Like a still life flower
tucked beneath the sill

I am something of a
transient nature -

Tanto amor,   *so much love,*
me diste tu -   *you once gave me -*

Se marchitó y canto   *has since withered and I sing*
Ay yay yay, que lastima   *what a shame*

My husband
is gone -

Gone far from me
and I too am gone -

My petals fall to the ground
one by one -

Like drops of blood
from a shotgun.

I am so sorry.
I am such a stiff and skinny flower;

Pale and deathly
in the early fall -

My naked stem to see -
my wilting rose bud of a woman -

It never blooms
anymore -

I cannot breathe
anymore

Por eso   *this is why*
te digo   *I tell you*

Me marcho hoy -   *today I go -*
subiendo, subterrizandome   *down, down, under the ground*

Sin ti, sin algunos   *without you, and without*
pétalos mas a sostenerme   *any more petals to sustain me*

Flor chiquita;   *little lost flower;*
yo se perder   *knows how to lose*

Pero ay yay yay...   *but, oh dear, oh my...*
como me duele   *how it hurts*

Sola una mujer,   *I am only a woman*
sea como la flor -   *I am just like the rose -*

Totalmente desnuda -   *completely naked -*
así soy yo, sin tu amor.   *how I've become, without your love.*

WHAT I SEE IN THE WATER
1938

I am that which has gotten so wet
Crazy as the man who begs for me

The water has gifted me sisters
With so much black hair, black vulcanized sisters

The Mexican earth, kills me like a bird
Kills me like a flower, and Popocatepetl

Consummates herself, then eats me - instinctively
Makes, demands of me: give her the water -
The water which reminds me

Of the goddamn past of mine - my parents still floating -
They are never of stone, rather pumice, as if from another planet

I notice married folks get smaller every single day
Every time which they

Arrive in my dreams - I cower and yellow down
My brown tone - I don the native slippers (such a good girl)

Their polio victim. And I drink their blood, blue veins like wine
From Mexico City, I am grey as smog makes the air
                                                without the love of a man

Nor a friend to call my own, nor a sister - she's no longer loyal

Nor my buried kin; they have gone down under the

Volcano. Insufferable - this is -
Takes a shit - its ash implies itself -
Excuses the belch - disgusting, so hateful

This is my mouth - which you are hoping to fill
To reform, the issues of our elders

Change in the wind, at the whim of God... of God's piss -
Small ones
Swim around my knees - in the yellow bath/soup

They stay under, inspecting every part of me
Docile hands - wavering like flag skins underwater -

                    This, what the water gives me. (not) Hope.

HIM AND ME (THE BASE SKULL)
1938

The teeth are what get at me.
The whiteness and the bone.

So happy - such a grinner -
This cut neck debaser -

To taste a young girl's life
And take from it from her with such

Pleasure.
So young, uninitiated,

She was;
She trembles

At this age - not understood by the mind;
Ni por su cuerpo   *neither her body*

Tratará de comprender   *can possibly understand*
Such a mouth, it's

Grin-bone. Su complejidad,   *his complexity*
Su sangre rojo; y su magia -   *red blooded magic -*

Su mente negro - contra   *his black mind - versus*
El pajarito amarillo   *the little yellow bird*

With its three little toes -
It flies in and out of

The vacated eye holes
Its caves and its deep holds -

It scrapes
Along her wing -

More wounded each
Time - y pregunto   *time - and I ask*

Así sería el camino, querido?

                              is this how the journey will be, my darling?

A Dios. O   *to God*
A Diablo.   *or to the Devil*

That grin, makes me
Feel

Like he has taken some-
Thing that was not his; and

How do you make a
Little girl's mind clean again,

Es que solo de   *it is only from*
The grey base skull.

The gap-toothed grin;
In the skin, dyed ochered;

So sickly, the colors
And so flawed -

The remains.

THE BALLAD OF DOROTHY HALE
1938

When falling out a window
the moon
wants to seduce me

Make love to me once more -
gravity confused as she falls -

Her husband left her
in anguish; harm.

I am painting tragedy
that's my blood
upon her face

Mujeres   fall   *women*
downdowndown

       Ejectable

I paint the tragedy,
as makeup, as blood -
look, it's already happening:

This Carnival of the dead in my town:
balloons, sick candy
goes up and down la calle   *the street*

Hago la feria de bruja   *I host the witch carnival*
underground;
muscles of meat;
the bodies succumb

Death himself arrives - he is surprised
at the good work he's done

Insects, rats engaged
luego sucio, luego basura   *later dirty, later garbage*
descomponiéndose   *decomposing*

Liquifies
bajo un sol sucio.   *under the filthy sun.*

This is how she kills herself:
the angled fractures
plus a puzzle of her spine

And how the sun
becomes the marriage garrison

The moon - a lesbian
monkey woman

Y yo – también estoy muriendo   *and I - I too am also dying*

The prison is also the body.
The divorce papers almost dry.

She whispers
make love to me once more?

Princesa del pavimento   *princess of the pavement*
could not convince a man---
to stay or to go; all I know -

In the ballad of Dorothy Hale

Is to mix the white and red for
her makeup, or for her blood
dab it upon her face

Or upon the terrible ground
for when I paint this tragedy

Woman falls down.

El Reloj (The Clock)
1938

Tick/tock
marca el reloj   *goes this clock*

No puedo continuar así   *I can't continue on like this*
contigo   *with you*

Con el dolor del tiempo   *with the pain of time*
destruyendo   *eating away*

mi corazón, mi mente.   *my heart, my mind*

Tu, yo, Lupe,
Christina, you and me,
your wife, my sister

Tantas dedos   *so many fingers*
me están haciendo sufrir   *they are making me suffer*

Me dejas / me consumes   *you leave / consume me*
you've made me yours

A viajar en tus mares,   *I swim in your seas*
oliendo los colores   *smell the colors*
hecho por un torso masculino   *made by your body*

Ésta divina tentación   *this divine temptation*
hace mis muslos temblar   *makes my muscles tremble*

a love bandage, my soul less hollow
my face more colorful;

En este teatro   *in this theater you*
eres la principal atracción.   *are the main attraction.*

From the weight of my legs I cannot
stand. You do not care enough - these

Stoic days of leaves and language.
Desde otoño hasta la primavera   *from autumn until spring*

Eso no es divertido   *this isn't even funny*
not that I judge, yet behold a
woman's seethe

Permeates my canvas my house my pores,
this skin wrap - ever present

Damp with mildew stench,
unbeknownst

Before I knew of this clock; and
your capable hands,

Que se van tick/tock   *the hands which go*
y lo que hicieran a mi.   *and what they would do to me.*

Mujer y Mono (Woman and Monkey)
1938

Nothing should end this violently:
Baby monkeys slide in and out

Of their madres - like the slippery pea pods   *mothers -*
So gently -

The wind sabe como tocar   *the wind knows how to touch*
A woman's cheeks

As if they could break her open
Hack easily at the insides of a body

So permanently destroy her -

But they do not. They take wing
Hovering

With their light hued lips in all the
Ripe flowers

Pistil and stamen alone except for this vigil
So abundant
So giving

With the nectar they make all life - all Edens
All the flying and the crawling and the stinging things

All snakes.
The thorns of Jesus know no harm
Except for when I am wearing it

As a necklace / as a hat
It's a choice to make.

Whilst I hold the ghost of my baby
Up to the Lord

The eyes of a
Mother begging for change on
The cathedral crumble steps

And in an offering of peace,
I remember.

Hurt Comes in Pairs
1939

There is a woman of the dirt.
And another.

Two nudes in the earth. Just
Me and my sister.

Look how she coils
Into my belly asking for

Forgiveness. I like to see her

Writhe like a worm, and
I step on her

Sometimes - to remind
Her of her smallness -

And how it feels to die.

And yet
She eats of my stomach, and
I keep her alive.

We are family
After all. But family is not
Good meat; it

Can kill you if allowed to
Fester such as this -

And if such meat is left
Unattended - such as this
Near your spouse's mouth

He might eat her alive
With utter delight and leave none
For anyone else -

He will be filled with the
Protein of her; her

Red celled goodness;
Meanwhile you are anemic; you are
Weak, and breathless -

You faint
Walking to the bathroom
Keeling at the waist

While her loin resides in the
Mouth of

A greedy king.
He is kneeling at her waist -

Who do I tell this to?

No one has prepared any
Dinner for me,

Y el olor de la carne   *and the smell of the meat*
Ya no lo soporto -   *I cannot tolerate -*

I paint myself with very short hair
And go to sleep with my monkey.

Mejores Amigas (Best Friends)
1939

Shunt shunt
Shut the fuck up

Stitch snip
Make a monster

Out of my heart
The blood fluent

In loss - in losing
Her man; the only thing

It knew, was how
To be happy wearing

Legs which didn't work
And a spine made of metal

Little paloma grows wings
Out of a dress of white

Flies inside the mouth
Of a friend

Makes a muscular nest
Eats red, creates

A new woman
Who is more perfect for you.

CORONA DE LA CÁRCEL (LACE JAIL)
1940

Lace encompasses
Or chokes the life

Out of something
So pure; my lace jail

Te miro desde adentro	*I see you from the inside*
Como si tu fueras	*as if you were*
El invierno	*the winter*
De mi cárcel	*of my jail*
Sufro aquí,	*I suffer here,*
Viviendo para ti	*living for you*
Comiendo ratas	*eating the rats*
de pura raza	*of pure race*
Por qué,	*because,*
Por qué.	*because.*

Must I be half
Of anything

La mitad	*half*
La mitad	*half*

No me siento   *I don't feel*
Como si fuera la mitad de algo   *like half of anything*

I want to be Frida
Just Frida. Artista.

Not any mix
Of any women

Nor any fantasy
Of your mind.

Pelón (Bald)
1940

Muy, muy, pero muy

such a very masculine woman

Masculina

So you don't think you will
Get to touch a woman anymore

You can lick a moustache
Touch my testicles

Fondle this traje estúpido

fondle my ridiculous suit

El que antes te gustaba verme puesto

the one you used to like me in

Lo hipersexual que me hiciste

the hypersexual you made me

La encadenada a la selva

the shackle of the jungle

Vestida con mi traje indigena

with my native dress upon my body

Calas blancas convertidas en basura

white calas, now they are looking like trash

Esta negra es pesada, pero liberada

heavy, this dark woman, but freed

Luciendo su corona de la cárcel y mucho más

wearing the crown of the jail, and is much more

De alguien más caballero que tú -

of a gentleman than you -

Gordo old viejo keep painting

fat old man just keep on painting

Mujeres con cabello largo

women with their long hair, so feminine - just how you like it

Tan femeninas como te gustan.

Y mira como las serpientes vienen a mi

and look how the snakes slither to me

Covering the floor like

All the men's fingers.

Amiga Mia (My Friend)
1940

Ultimately
It's the bed

And me, in it, or upon it
The length of it: or short way -

I would climb under
It if I could

De hecho,   *in fact,*
I would make love to it

Abrade its mahogany limbs
With my skin, trash talk it till
It gives in, goes to foot and holds

Me down
De vez en cuando, me imagino   *every now and then, I imagine*
Que la cama me habla--   *that the bed talks to me --*

Frida, me dice   *Frida, she says*

*Siéntate sin ropa, en mi cara, enséñame cómo hacerte sentir
como una mujer*
    sit on my face without clothes, teach me how to make you feel like a woman

Cama idiota, le digo:

bed, you idiot, I say, you are but made of wood, and I am of skin

ya sabes que eres de
Maduro, y yo soy de piel,

Is it not...? she counters,

My forest muscle showing...?
Is it not...? your city muscle showing...?

Así es de verdad, y te das cuenta,

so it is... and you realize, that the bed actually knows things,

que la cama de hecho sabe cosas

Importantes e intrínsecas del mundo.

important and intrinsic about the world.

When I paint
She watches me,
Languishing.

When I
Touch myself there,

She rocks and groans,
gripped in the throes of
lo sensual.   *the sensual.*

Supongo que the bed

es mi amiga y mi novia.

I suppose the bed is my friend and my lover.

I tell her
hold me up, old friend

While I quiver in the heat of
my dreams

Hold me down, she says,
whilst I

Witness your
orgasmic screams.

La Última Cena (The Last Supper)
1940

Si mi propia mesa   *if my own table*
Fuera something   *was something*
Like Jesus's bread
Breaking moment;

Si la mesa de Dios   *if God's table*
Fuera something   *was something*
Like God's arms
Wrapping around me -

Rather than white
Trunks of hellish
Divination -

How the owning of me
Mi gente? My little   *my people?*
Deer, son mis babies,   *they were my babies,*

Mucho más -   *so much more -*

My loss, and
Melancholy -

In the blood
And in the food
Served for no one

87

Else than that cracked

Cabeza - es un rostro   *split head - did it to myself*
Of my own making.

Yo, le esperaba a la cena -   *I have withstood - all these years*
Yo, comia con Diego   *eating beside him*
Compartiendo el pan   *sharing stale bread with him*
Consigo -

Como si fuera   *as if he was Jesus*
Jesús, o su fantasma   *or the ghost of Jesus*

Ya no compartiré -   *I don't want to share anymore -*
Con ninguno -   *with anybody -*
Como que yo soy   *for I am*
La Crucificada -   *the crucified woman -*

I'M ALL THAT'S LEFT
1940

Frida Trotsky.
American starlet.
Russian communist.
Mexican traitor,

Liberate the masses.
Famous paintress,
Humble housewife.
Diva dancing the night,
Illustrious

Chef.
Princess.

Artist of the face.
Frida, mujer -   *woman -*
No Rivera,
No flowing stride
No white dress.

Muted help of the hills.
German yet so very Mexican.
So very native -

So much a hybrid
My pollen needs are varied and provocative.

I am provocateur.

Suffrage,
Woman of the hill and mountain.
Woman of the pyramid.

The lake bed quetzal calls to me in dreams
They tried so many times to roll my head down the stairs
To see how many times I would get up and survive.

I've outlived them all. Enslavers, cannibals, rapists.
I'm all that's left of the carnage.

No tengo país   *I have no country*
No tengo raza   *I have no race*

Ni lengua   *nor language*
Ni color ---   *nor color ---*

Soy Calderón de la Tierra: *I am of the Earth:*

Naked.
Alone.

Flower Seller
1941

On the asphalt I go
To Acapulco
Past the rubble; burned tires,
El agua 'no potable'   *signs for "don't drink the water"*

A family, a girl, their roses,
Tantas calas   *so many calla lilies for sale*
White pinafore; white linen
I can smell her youth changing over to woman

The burro tied
The Fiat parked

I walk across the black tar flat
To ask: *cuánto cuesta una docena*   *how much for a dozen*
Me dice: *pa'a usted Señor,*   *and she tells me, for you sir,*
Solo ciento-cincuenta.   *only $150.*

Miracles - these flowers
To my wife I get on one knee
Tell her - eres toda,   *I tell her, you are everything,*
Completamente todo para mi   *absolutely everything to me*

But the girl
By the road
Was in white
Her hair tight

Behind the nape
Her arched neck
Like a child

With the bouquet of callas
I cannot taste these offerings
Yet the existence of her beauty

Hangs like an odor
of me wanting her everywhere.

Pensando en Diego (Thinking About Diego)
1940-43

Climbing the pyramid in Teotihuacan
You tell me you love me as
A man falls ten steps; his

Arm badly broken
Hikes the rest of the way back down
The steep stairs
With his son, who is crying

We shrug and make-out
Tongue tied babies
Nineteen-year-old playmates
Measuring the world in hotels and
Dancing

Later at El Museo de Arqueológico   *the archaeology museum*
Me dices: *you say to me;*
quiero subirte en la cripta y   *I want to hide you in the crypt*
Hacerte el amor   *and make love to you*

It's the best thing I've ever heard
Make love as only
A Mexican can

Selfish,
Incessant,
With lips

To die for.

I paint you upon my eyebrow
So you will remember me
Un tatuaje de la vida que   *a tattoo of the life which*
Que tuvimos antes, hace tiempo.   *we once had together, before.*

And there goes the man with his
Boy; full arm cast in white, they
Are looking at artifacts from the
Time of Quetzalcoatl

And you and I smile at each other
And kiss.
We kiss till it feels like a strangle.

Self-Portrait as Tehuana
1943

I peek out

I am crying

Tears of silver or diamonds or pearls

Back again to the half / I am cut in half by so many hands so
many clocks and voices, I hear yours the most clearly even
when you don't tell me directly, when you touch her thigh I
realize - I should have worn the vestido nativo, when you
caressed the sides of her small pert breasts, I remember I
should cook more, or wear a crown of flowers, or paint you
upon my chest ---

I seek out

Begging

Your attention - my man, my love, my muralist

Why do I care? What purpose this dedication… this art and
lovemaking - me and you, is an always thing --- and yet surely
a never, if not, why would you do this to me? Why would you
dress me up in linens yet take her to bed instead of me?
You do things like this. Like this. Why would you take off my
skin and leave me standing there? In the road. Cold. And so
alone. With neither dress on.

I stare out

Suffering

Woman cut into two identities, and I with my face supplicating at your feet

Sometimes I like to let the roots drag me back to the trees, just to get away from you, and your opinion of me - but when I do, when I drag her over the earth, the dirt is as cruel as your lips can be --- so I return to the prior method of judging my own worth in how many times you've kissed her.

I fall down

Asking -

How is this possible – that my husband could do this to me.

La Mujer muy Asunder
(The Woman Fallen Asunder)
1943

If I were an animal being eaten alive by a snake
I would not tell it to stop for I would not want
The chance of my death to be put at risk; pain
In different ways can be seen as endless or never-
Ending, any way you look at it - a way to feed some
Other being with the blood and rotten meat of one's
Carcass - what else shall these puzzle pieces be if
Not nectar for the humble hummingbird; she flies,
Selfless, sips of my nectar, makes a small nest and
Deposits her three precious ova; mine are three
Million and then some, fetid stench of road-kill
Jaguar, her uterus punctured by the bus's axle;
Three small kittens in her sanguine room, shrivel
And whine, whelped babes with no mother - mother
Is prone - made useless as creator - unless she
Is consumed by a half-starving predator who,
Without the gift of her muscle, would have also
Been made moot - flaccid and exiled, mi cuerpo
Never given a chance to feed another - left to
Rot in the sun, su carne non-fecund; sus tetas
Nunca dan la leche a ningún hijo ni están tran-
quila in the earth --- but my body torn siempre

muy asunder.

*(her non-fecund meat, her nipples, never gave milk to any child nor can she
be calm in the earth, with her body always torn so asunder.)*

Soy La Tierra (I am the Earth)
1943

In my bed I flow forth from the naked Earth
over hills and valleys once conquered by Cortez
Los Mestizos work to regain the dirt;

those having both Spanish and indigenous descent

Poblanos climb to rid el piramide or the horrid

poblanos - people from Puebla, MX

chapel, bone building of Christ, his thorns make
scars down our backs, the sliding down, the demolishing of
Catholic peaks and turrets; from whence

They exalted Hallelujah, los chiflados are dead and mired

their leaders

in ground, their horses are ours, their mercados

their markets free for the taking

libre for the taking by us white dressed, mustache-
twirlers hell bent on circumventing el Día de los Muertos;
queriendo nuestra tierra y nuestras bellas mujeres

wanting our earth and our beautiful women

Mira como yo vengo negrita de la Nación; marrón

look at me arrive; the dark-skinned woman of our Nation;
brown and with green arms of the jungle

y con verdes brazos de la selva; I am your Mother;
I am not Christ's mother, not immaculate in any way
but in death I give birth, impregnated by my favorite
shoot; handsome its veins and masculine its twine
feel it seismic from my hips; mira the explosion

of life and the gifts of my womb, once broken-
inert - my blood manifests life for an entire continent -

I don't sell bananas for overseas markets; this is
grown in the hills of my very own pocket, my
primitive dress houses a million male rockets, but look
how I manage the phallic creep - one leaf
one life - one baby - one vine - out of my body
comes la Resistencia - juvenile deities fold to
my Madonna, and I become a quetzal - a phoenix
I rise from los granos - make green the world

I rise from the grains -

then open my dress for the world to peer in.

Flower of Life
1943

My parchment opens slowly
due to humid days
the frosted dark

The fabric of my body cloth
thick veined, slow, unable

Why open at all -
why give so much pollen
when it's the world
at me, sneezing

Spreading germs
I have given up my middle
bud, again and again

Yet God. The tempting
smell of wood. The
simmering of bees

He planned for Eden
well, so well

That never a woman
could resist a snitching snake
a rotting apple.

Nor can I
the flit of

Spring, the waft of
flowers deep in sexual
trading. So, God

You want me in the Garden.
Fine. I'm coming

Spraying yellow dust at you,
and you
and you,

Don't waste me
wither and yawn, this mayday sun

Let you lick each granule as I quiver
from within.

ACHE AND BLOSSOM
1943

Fire shooting
Molten crimson
Black and grey; I ruminate

And twinge -
Belly rupture
Arctic yellow
Small animals chew
On my sinews

Dam of green orange
Stains of ocher
Slide knives inside
The belt.

No sheathe
No scabbard
Only my pelvis

To capture the metal
Deathly white shines over the gilt cage

God's skin porous
God's runny eyes

He cannot walk to save
His hide - yet

I can walk
To my
Canvas

And if not - I'll create one
From my bedside

The pink lips of the flower
Spilling rouge magenta;
Fragrant drips
Of my rose

Healing my bones -
Spilling water -
I paint and drip and burn -
A deep ache, and blossom.

Palomas Like Me (Flame Flower)
1943

I am a man / a woman -
soy homosexual / soy lesbiana

el ímpetu de tí / your motivation
lush wetness / such dreams

me canse de los negocios   *I am so tired of what men need*
with men; their many
parts

todos ellos piden mucha   *they all want so much*
atención   *attention*

yet look at the woman
in the fabled twilight -

on my arm,
on my chest
sitting on my penis

I am erect / she is stark upright

no tengo duda   *I have no doubts*
no tengo verguenza   *I have no shame*

if I am going to be a barren
woman, with a cheating husband

then I shall make love to my
own hag harem / I shall eat her nectar

I shall dance the tango
& wax her crescent moon

y yo seré   *and I will be*
the instigator / for

I am so much woman -
ven, y mírame -   *come and look at me -*

how I glow / how I effervesce
and bloom.

Columna (Spinal Column)
1944

I bear within the prodding
Menace; it is a combination
Of public and private
Discomfort. I wear it as a corset.
I heed your penis so far inside
Me it tastes like food and becomes
Sustainable though the metallic
Piercing of it excruciating,
Something horrible as a child's dream
I would not wish on anyone - especially
When so young, in bed colors bleed
Into one thing - one giant red head
Which pulses throbs behind my eyes.
When I open my mouth there is
El serpiente behind my teeth
When I say your name I sputter
Black letters - d.i.e.g.o.
De morir is to love is to   *to die*
Live through death
To sustain is to paint
Is to use one's art like a crutch
When I am alone I count
Stitches, bones, surgeries, hours
Colors, butterflies, peacocks, dogs
I count the years I would have been
Dead. Since riding the bus.
Deformed. Since consummating our marriage.

Lo Que Somos
(What We Are)
1929-1944

Somos eso que vuela hacia el sol

we are the thing which flies to the sun

Quemado - falls charred and broken, back to the earth

burned -

The thing which evokes the tantalizing jaguar, makes a trap

Hides the bone then eats it himself;
cazado es el cazador   *hunted becomes the hunter*

So many times, I lost you as my lover - so many times

The way my heart came out of my body as you went to her
side

Las mujeres de tu vida are like food to you -

the women of your life

they make you full

They make you strong - so excellent for your health:
look how robust and older

We are the men of jovial pride. I am a man; I could have
been; I

Longed to be - for I too would have fallen in love with me -

Danced with women half my age; felt their lithe arms around
my waist

Turned their chins to the moonlight to kiss them - to use them;

I cannot escape you. Look at how we have become the same
thing -
this entwining of the arteries

The operation to separate our skulls; our zippered torsos at
the seams - must

Kill us: ancient, freak couple: decrepit and broken - my whole
stupid life

Paloma tuya - volando arriba, en el cielo, para siempre,

                 your dove - I fly above you, in heaven, forever,

Diego Rivera, you were always near the wheelchair.
You were my legs, my strength, my heart -

And I, your one and only dove.

La Magnolia y La Pera
(The Magnolia and The Pear)
1945

All white things are not only white
Some explode with asexual frivolity in

The Sonoran Desert twilight. Some faint at
The mention of Alejandro's thighs,

While some carry the pride of orgasmic
Delights at the hands of feminists on

Their vagina, on darkly nippled breasts
Fluttering petals making erect my skin

As if I were bequeathed as a child to Georgia
No a un viejo, gordo, infiel   *not to some old, fat, adulterer*

Who goes by the name
Of Diego.

THE CHICK
1945

Mushroom cloud vapor of hair, open my head and see the
spiders clamor for their share of this fracase; soft and yellow,
cruel is the zag; monument built on a pyramid of loose sticks.
Puebla defiled, mushroom bomb sits like Stalin on the back of
a broken country's bones, a little yellow puff, my little yellow
house: delicious, exposed, and the mantis prays, the quake
of cracking earth splits me open, crack runs from my cervix to
the tip of my tongue - the swallow of the bug and the spider
and the race and the poor and downtrodden.

The names which they assign us.... It's important to
remember - spiders often eat their mates after copulation.

MITI / MITI (HALF / HALF)
1945

Mírame	*look at me,*
Soy mitad mitad	*I am half / half*
Alive / dead	
Who can know?	

The parts incoming
Dead, I know
My friends, my pets
My skull - who can tell

My foot from the	
Wretched turkey claw	
Sopa de carne -	*meat soup -*
Borne of my intestines	

Dust of bone -
Broth of my bones
Held so much / wasted on the bus

And gone

Escúchame	*listen to me*
Soy mitad mitad	*I am half / half*
No mamá / Si hija -	*not mother / yes, a daughter -*
They tell me now	
How it could be of use to me	

Huesos / iron / protein /
Sus huesos dan vida   *your bones give life*
A mis huesos -   *to my bones -*

I don't want those babies'
Bones - they are but
Pups and kits and baby monkeys

Huéleme   *smell me*
Soy mitad mitad   *half / half*
Empty / full
Of the feces of animals
Of myself
Of children

I would eat if I felt
The hunger
But the only thing I feel is
Bloat - death

Siénteme   *feel me*
Soy mitad mitad   *half / half*
Frida con hambre / Frida tan satisfecha   *Frida hungry / Frida full*

In the bed / in the ground

Bloody
          waterfall
                    funneling

down.

El Paisaje Mexicano
1946

In the clouds, fists of water;
my listless earth -

wanes
grayer, bleaker -

her in-transient core -
I never imagined

could shrink or waver - while
the likes of Man,

their feats:
pernicious

their lies grow -
thicker, more alive and

full,
of power.

Mientras,   *meanwhile,*
my silken dunes

mi país - mi desierto -   *my country - my desert -*
a ver   *now look*

un esqueleto de mujer   *there is a skeleton of a woman*
soy yo   *it is me*

and a skull in the corner -
eres tu   *it is you*

o tal vez,   *or maybe,*
los dos sean - yo   *they are both - me*

quien sabes -   *who knows -*
ya viene   *here comes*

el dolor -   *the pain -*
me encantan los nopales   *I adore the nopales*

como si fueran mis bebes -   *as if they were my babies -*
sus caras, cambian mas a gris   *their faces, turning to gray*

the Silver Desert - la Ghost Madre   *mother*
de mi alma   *of my soul*

in my heart, she continues
crumbling, folding

over listless eyes - Dios -   *- God -*

I owe so much;

I owe such monies - I am

118

deeply lidded,

as I grow fruitless - this barren dirt
who can say - if

I am alive - in my art -
or if I am simply dying -

estoy cambiando   *I am changing*
a polvo   *into dust*

I am going to ground -
in my hurt.

Lo que Carma Hizo a mi Granizo
(What Karma Did to my Little Deer)
1946

Well this is the bitch of it all
Isn't it - when the NYC and the D.F.
Are really the same old thing - takes
Many prosperous men to codify the
Stacked disks of a spine - an M.D.
Doesn't really know which segment he
Should place where - for in school
They do not teach how to rebuild
Vertebrae - they only teach them to
Be doctors, to use bandaids and aloe
Salve, they are not sent to Europe to
Intern with Degas; they are at the mercy
Of Picasso prints which show the woman
As me - in many pieces - only a glue gun &
Several tins of tacks - a gurney -

This is war, this is mayhem, a Civil War
Graveyard. How many slivers and shards must one remove
To fund and rebuild an entire human? Can a foot
Really hold the weight again after
The iron ball from a cannon loves it
More than ever did its mother - see how it
Never gives in, never abandons its newest-
Friend - so many bones in a foot - better off
We could melt them down as a gelatinous glue and recast

The troublesome foot as a bovine hoof -

Less painful; more suitable; once it hardens
It will be something which even a painter
Could love, despite the immature mold -

Crudely cast by the underprepared
Medical school sculptors-
And the spine, well, we could scrape out the

Cylinder, right down to the
Bone and annulus - watch your eyes
For the sweet squirt of the nucleus-

Pour molten metal from the mouth
Down through to the anus.

MÉTODO DE TOCAR
(THE METHOD OF TOUCHING)
1949

Somos animales, más o menos

we are only animals - more or less

You summon, I come. You tell me
to stroke

I stroke. You mention your hands
are my hands under my dress,

I believe you. I want your mouth
more than food.

Your lips sate me
más que agua.   *more than water.*

I want to feel the pressure
of your weight crushing me,

Realigning me, I cannot support
your heft

It's much like the world
too wet and wild,

It's like the rain,

I lay flat

It does not pool,
It runs down

My sides as fingers
chase bugs

Never staying where I need
in place for health,

For pleasure.
Trace me.

Make me new.
Make a mural

Of my stomach.
Make me dance beautiful.

Coloca tu lengua.   *place your tongue.*
Coloca tu masculinidad.   *place your masculinity.*

Viaja a mis entrañas.   *go inside me.*
Te seguiré adonde vayas.   *I'll follow you anywhere.*

The way you kiss my face.
Mira como me haces temblar.   *look how you make me tremble.*

My body is an earthquake
I explode below the city.

You summon me.
I come to you.

Mi vestido blanco, my white dress
Mi cabello negro, my black hair

Larghissimo como me gustas.

so long, it is, I am the way you want me to be.

No cambias. I don't ask.

but you never change for me.

I am the changing thing.
I go to heaven in my mind.

You take my body there
when you want to

You carry me there,
sometimes.

The Dead Parts Don't Help Me
1951

I grip the brush
I do the strokes

I say names over and over
Diego Frida Papa Christina

See me move the bodies
around:

Frutas, verduras   *fruit, vegetables*
perritos, monitos   *puppies, baby monkeys*

I move things to suit my
viewing better

Settled in the bed; a wooden coffin.
A linen cover.

I cannot move the legs
for functioning better.

For viewing the canvas either.
That's why I bring

The things of life to me.
I am full of dead parts,

They do not move
anywhere,

In any way
to help me.

Aguantar: V. To Sustain, To Stand
1949

Dolor es algo como Dios -

pain is something like God -

Sovereign, powerful
Unyielding, unflinching.

Making decisions
Often, without thinking -

El dolor es como el amor

pain is something like love

Spellbinding, the feel of lips
Succulently nibbling -

Endless prickles and twangs in my thighs belly back uterus
Even my breasts - taut - heightened - hurting

El dolor es algo así como el fracaso -

pain is something like failure -

Can't pinpoint the loss
Can't tabulate how many fetuses gone
Only knowing they stack up to Heaven

One upon the next - chipped disks of a spine, the crumple-
black-rot -
In place of smooth pink, semi-gelatinous cartilage

Dolor es como de casar -

pain is something like getting married -

The husband who never leaves your side
The husband who grips and twists your spine

Sex, which penetrates your inner walls
As well hammers away at an insolent cervix - time after time
- after time -

El dolor, es como el castigo -

pain is something like punishment -

A broken wife - and he breaks things too;
The marriage vows, like tremors below the city -

Shaky, unsustainable
Like my pain - my balance -
Being upright - standing -
Unsustainable

Yet -
I have sustained, all of it,
Aún -

El dolor, es como aguantar todo -

pain is something like withstanding it all -

The word sustains - wraps around bones
Which wear the mask of the Devil?

130

Pain is like our love - which robbed me of as much
As it robbed me of - full - of myself - full of the blood
Of Diego – nosotros nos convertimos – el uno en el otro -

we become each other -

The pact - ears brimming with his semen
My pain - dragging me under the poisoned hood

I sit in my chair
The rest of my life -

Screaming at the sun.

THE FRUIT WHICH I PAINTED MATTERS TO ME
1953

Paloma   *dove*
I've always been
since the day we began -
like a mango from your mouth to mine
slippery and succulent;
piel y lengua - sabrosas   *succulent skin and tongue*
pajarita de tu boca -   *little bird in your mouth*
dulce, y blanca -   *soft, and white*

Paloma, soy.   *I am your dove.*
I've always ached
for peace, for my country
and from within my broken bones -

Es demasiado para poder dormir   *It's too much to sleep*
así - con tanto dolor, moriré

like this - with so much pain, better I die,

- algun día...   *- someday...*

Paloma   *dove*
wants to fly home now;
from my bed I can still see
out of the window - view the country I love

sus venas de la vida pulsan	*the veins of life are pulsing*
todavía - conmigo, o	*with or without me*
sin mi - no importa	*they will, either way*

except that the fruit that I painted
matters so much to me.

el papaya -	*the papaya -*
las venas	*the veins*
el cuerpo	*the body*
la muerte	*the death*
mi mente	*my mind*
ya vuela	*now flies*

y mucho más,	*and so much more,*
De tu Paloma; fue para ti	*from your Dove; was for you*

Diego.	
Mexico.	
Mundo.	*world.*
Adios.	*goodbye.*

Es la hora.	*it's my time.*
Libérenme.	*set me free.*

Doble Mujer
1954

Like ash

Vuelo al cielo -   *I fly to heaven -*
So light

A woman remade
In God's eyes

Blind to the hurt
The loss; little pockets of bliss

I have kept from you
Perfectly hatched

Mujer de nuevo.   *woman again.*
In God's darkening eyes
Sin peso   *weightless*

I am reinvented -
I float above you

Like ash.

Prior Acknowledgements

Flower Seller, Chantarelle's Notebook

Mejores Amigas, Pelado, Neon Mariposa Magazine

Magnolia y la Pera, Rabid Oak

Proyecto para Repararme en Tres Etapas, Vol II, Moonchild Magazine

KEY TO THE POEMS/PAINTINGS

Corona de la Cárcel	Self Portrait, 1948
Pelón	Self-Portrait With Cropped hair, 1940
Amiga Mia	Amiga Mia TheDream (The Bed), 1940
La Última Cena	The Wounded Table, 1940
I'm All That's Left	Self-Portrait with Braid, 1941
Flower Seller	Flower Seller (Rivera), 1941
Pensando en Diego	
	The Love Embrace of the Universe, the Earth (Mexico),
	Myself, Diego, and Señor Xolotl, 1949
Self Portrait as Tehuana	Self Portrait as Tehuana, 1948
La Mujer muy Asunder	
	Self-Portrait with Thorn Necklace and Hummingbird, 1940
Soy La Tierra	Roots, 1943
Flower of Life	Still Life Round, 1942
Ache and Blossom	Self-Portrait, Dedicated to Dr. Eloesser 1940
Palomas Like Me	Fruit of Life, 1953
Columna	The Broken Column, 1944
Lo que Somos	Diego and Frida, 1944
La Magnolia y La Pera	Magnolias, 1945
The Chick	El Pollito, 1945
Miti Miti	Without Hope, 1945
El Paisaje Mexicano	Landscape, 1946
Lo que Carma hizo a mi Granizo	The Wounded Deer, 1946
Método de Tocar	Diego and Frida, 1944
The Dead Parts Don't Help Me	
	Self-Portrait with the Portrait of Doctor Farill,1951;
	Thinking About Death, 1943
Aguantar: v. To Sustain, To Stand	Diego and I, 1949
The Fruit Which I Painted Matters to Me	Weeping Coconuts, 1951
Doble Mujer	The Mask, 1945

Acknowledgements

Thank you to my family - my husband Josh, and my sons Peter and Thomas, for enduring the times when Mommy is lost in her head writing poems. I love you so much.

Thank you to the wonderful Cephalopress, my dear publishers, for taking a chance on this project. I'm not sure any of us, Dave, Maté, Stina, or even I could imagine how the book would take on a life of its own, and grow and morph over an entire year until now. The editors at Cephalo have given me such trust, understanding and care, as I would keep sending more and more poems, through difficult edits and organization, and the completion of the full Spanish translation over this last spring and summer. This has been such an epic undertaking for me, and I thank my editors for giving me the space and time to work through this book. I struggled endlessly to make this book as perfect and as real a tribute to Frida as I could possibly manage.

Thank you to my mom and dad, Carol and Richard, and my sisters, Catherine and Anne, for your endless support and unconditional love. For always believing in me, even when I didn't believe in myself.

Thank you to John Homan and Jorge Montero Calderón for their brilliant edits to my very flawed Spanish and their gentle guidance.

Thank you to my friend and Press Manager Amanda McLeod for her patience, guidance, proofreading and organization. You keep me together, lovely.

Thank you to Robert Kenter for his love and support as I wrote these poems and healed from my surgery.

Thank you to James Diaz - soul poet friend, for always holding out a hand in the darkness, and for never letting go. I love you.

Finally, thank you to you, Frida Kahlo, for your life, your art, your deep beauty and brilliant mind. I am humbled to dedicate this book to you - and I hope beyond measure that I might have made you pleased with my words. I carry you in my soul always, and thank you for helping me through my own pain, loss, and ultimate healing, while finding the strength in the creation of my poetry, as you showed me how to do, with your paintings.

With love and gratitude, Eli

About the Author

Elisabeth Horan is a poet from Vermont, advocating for animals, children and those suffering alone and in pain - especially those ostracized by disability and mental illness.

She is Editor-in-Chief at Animal Heart Press, and Co-Editor at Ice Floe Press. She has several chaps and collections out this year including *Bad Mommy / Stay Mommy* at Fly on the Wall Press, *Odd list Odd house Odd me* at Twist It Press, *Was It R*pe*, from Rhythm and Bones Press, and *Just to the Right of the Stove*, with Hedgehog Poetry Press.

She is a poetry mentor and proud momma to Peter and Thomas.

Follow her @ehoranpoet
& ehoranpoet.com

Made in the USA
Monee, IL
24 August 2022

12358053R00089